ALLIGATORS CAN'T STAND Butterflies

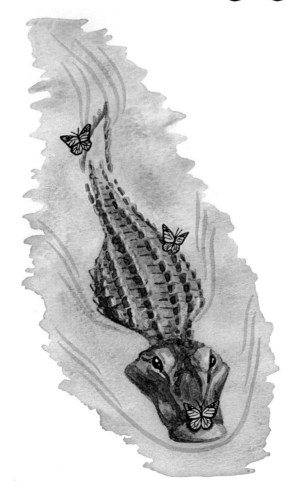

STORY BY
KEITH LAWRENCE ROMAN

STORY EDITING BY
MARY LOU ROMAN

ILLUSTRATIONS BY
SUMMER JOY CLANCY

Morningside Books

Morningside Books Trade Paperback Edition

Published in the United States of America by
Morningside Books, Orlando, Florida

This edition is cataloged as:
ISBN 978-0-9827288-3-3

www.MorningsideBooks.net

Printed in the United States of America

INTRODUCTION

There is a stretch of seashore along the Gulf of Mexico, within the boundaries of Florida, known as The Forgotten Coast. Beginning at the mouth of the Aucilla River and continuing in a southwest direction to the point of land at Cape San Blas, then turning northwest to Mexico Beach, the Forgotten Coast is for the most part a scruffy unshaven beard on the land. While a few places along this part of the Florida coast, such as barrier islands, contain beautiful white sand beaches, most of the Forgotten Coast consists of thick saltwater marshes. These marshes serve as nurseries for tiny aquatic life. They are also the starting point of a food chain supporting creatures as small as shrimp and as large as eagles.

A part of this coast has been divided off as a safe harbor or refuge for thousands of unique species of plants and wildlife. The area, which includes 68,000 acres of freshwater ponds, saltwater marsh, and woodland, is named the Saint Marks National Wildlife Refuge. There are 552 National Wildlife Refuges in the United States, each quite different from all the others. There are wildlife refuges in wilderness areas that include the tops of mountains and others that consist of tropical islands and the waters that surround them. All of the refuges share a common theme: that any animal who lives there and any plant that grows there is safe from being hunted or picked by humans.

White-tailed deer

Inside the St. Marks Wildlife Refuge are four types of environments. Most of the land is slightly raised above the water, and filled with tall longleaf pine, short saw palmetto scrub and white oak woods. This is very different from the almost 50 miles of saltwater marsh coastline that also belongs to the refuge. A special feature that makes the St. Marks Refuge attractive, especially to birds who have come south for the winter, are the dozen or so large freshwater man-made ponds, which act as a bridge between the sea and the forest, and are home to a wide menagerie of creatures. These ponds were built by workers with the specific plan of creating winter homes for migratory birds such as ducks and geese. The marshes in the freshwater pools gather rainwater and help drain it to the Gulf of Mexico while offering food and shelter to many different kinds of animals and birds.

Longleaf pine

If you were to walk very quietly along the old timber trails through the saw palmetto and slash pine woodlands of the refuge, so as to not be heard, you would almost always surprise one or two white-tailed deer, a family of bandit-masked raccoons, or perhaps a black wild sow with her tiny black piglets. But as sneaky as you might be, you still would not surprise any of the Florida black bears living in the St. Marks Refuge woodlands. Bears are out there, but their ability to smell a newcomer from far away and their shyness of humans keeps them out of sight. You may be fortunate enough to see a few of their large-clawed paw prints.

Black wild sow with piglets

Be careful as you walk the narrower trails so as not to brush against a wild American holly tree or a prickly pear cactus. These are plants that scratch and sting.

Wild American holly

Prickly pear cactus

Learn how to identify poison ivy and avoid touching it, to prevent a blistery, itchy rash. Stay on the marked trails so you prevent unpleasant encounters with these plants and spend more time enjoying the birds, animals, insects, and plants of the refuge.

Poison ivy

While in the woods, take time to look closely at the upper branches of the pine trees. You may be rewarded with the sight of a bald eagle nest! These large nests are scattered throughout the forest. Every so often, one of the grown eagles will leave its nest to soar above the woodland and freshwater ponds, heading toward the gulf front waters. The eagle will cross over miles of coastal marsh in just a few minutes. Once there, if the tide is right, the eagle will find a meal of mullet or other shallow saltwater fish.

American bald eagle nest

If the eagle finds the fishing poor that day, a blue-winged teal duck or another water bird like an American coot paddling across a nearby freshwater pond may find itself taken as a replacement dinner. As the bald eagle crosses the two mile long expanse of dark green-brown needle rush, it passes over a blue crab paddling underwater to catch a meal of tiny pink shrimp. With its telescopic vision, the eagle sees every periwinkle snail on every blade of the grasslike rushes. Savannah sparrows cower in the grassy brush. Flounder bury themselves in the muddy bottom, equally afraid of being caught by the eagle. These seas of grasses and rushes are home for thousands of inhabitants, most of which are likely to be supper for larger predator animals.

Blue crab with pink shrimp

Many of those predators are visitors from the nearby freshwater ponds. Here live American alligators and anhingas, river otters and osprey. The huge 1000-acre ponds were created in the 1930s by the formation of large earthen dikes. The dikes run for miles, with the sides forming the banks of the giant man-made lakes and the tops serving as trails for rangers and visitors. Visitors can walk along the tops of these levees, which are wide enough to support a car or truck and covered with mowed green grass. People walking along these elevated trails that rise a dozen feet above the water level are likely to see as many wild animals as found on a trip up the Amazon River or on an

River otter

African plains safari. Of course, the creatures who make their homes in the St. Marks Refuge are in a "jungle" of their own.

In the ponds of the St. Marks Wildlife Refuge, or for that matter any low-lying body of water in the southeastern United States, the king of the swamp is the American alligator. Thousands of alligators live at the St. Marks Refuge. Most are between eight and twelve feet long. With their huge jaws filled with sharp teeth and long-scaled tails, these fierce

American alligator

creatures resemble dinosaurs more than other small reptiles such as the many varieties of turtles living in the refuge. The alligator's long tail works as a propeller as it silently slides through the water of the refuge freshwater ponds. If all goes well for the gator that day it will capture in its mighty jaws a small duck such as an American wigeon, or a bluegill fish.

American wigeons

Usually the many species of ducks at St. Marks, such as the green-winged teal and the Northern pintail, quickly spot danger in the form of a half-submerged alligator, or a red-shouldered hawk diving down from the sky. Once alert and alarmed, the ducks, geese and wading birds such as the little blue herons that make their home in these ponds, quickly take flight. The blue-winged teal and coots fly in large flocks, circling the pond several times before landing, still together, hundreds of yards away from the danger. Of course a loud voice or too heavy a footstep will just as quickly send the ducks into the sky.

Red-shouldered hawk

But, a cruising alligator or visitors making noise may not be the only reasons the ducks take flight. Look to the sky to spot predators such as a Northern harrier (a hawk that flies low over the ponds and marshes) or a yellow-clawed bald eagle circling higher above.

Visitors to the St. Marks Refuge who have binoculars can peer through the lenses to see another world on the far side of the freshwater ponds. There, along the wooded shore where the inland forest begins, live great egrets and tri-colored herons who fish among the duckweed and cattails. The wading birds must compete with creatures from the forest such as raccoons and even bears for a dinner of the bass or shellcrackers that hide in the bulrushes and other wetland plants.

Egret catching a shellcracker

Still, those feathered birds and furry animals do not rule the St. Marks ponds. The American alligator does. With its ability to swim quickly across the ponds and crawl about on land, the gator is the terror of this small world. However, the kingdom of the alligator does not go too far past the trees. Gators seldom travel far from water and the elevated terrain of the St. Marks Refuge soon changes from marsh to woodlands filled with tall longleaf pines. Nesting in these trees are eagles and osprey. Also making a home in the longleaf pine forests of St. Marks are the endangered red-cockaded woodpeckers. These small woodpeckers chip away at the trunks of the longleaf pine, digging under the bark while searching for spiders, roaches, tree ants, and insect eggs to eat. Once they finish their excavation, the hollowed out spot becomes a home for other small creatures such as Carolina chickadees, mice and families of different types of woodpeckers. There is a separate world high above the ground, in the trees of the St. Marks Wildlife Refuge.

Red-cockaded woodpecker

On the ground beneath the nests of birds are white-tailed deer leaping over the scrub and brush. The deer travel for miles seeking out the softest sweetest sprouts of leaves and grass. At night, opossums will scurry from tree to tree in the moonlight, staying hidden as if on a secret mission. Gray squirrels in their nests are usually sleeping while raccoon families go on fishing and berry hunting expeditions. The Florida black bears that have made the refuge their home push and plow their way through both the darkness and the saw palmetto bushes. There are tens of thousands of forested acres in the St. Marks Wildlife Refuge. All of these are a protected habitat for the Florida black bears and other animals who live there.

Added to the saltwater marsh, freshwater ponds and wooded forests of the St. Marks Wildlife Refuge is one more very different type of territory. This is a place carved from the wildness almost 200 years ago. On a small point of land one mile south of the mouth of the St. Marks River sits a painted white brick tower made by men to guide tall sailing ships safely through the sea. That is the St. Marks Lighthouse. The light has sent its beacon across the curve of the earth since 1837. Visitors stroll along the grass paths on the grounds around the lighthouse and its connected building, seldom realizing that hundreds of years ago Spanish explorers landed here in a vast wilderness in search of New World treasures.

The lighthouse and the land surrounding it are a tamed animal in the middle of untamed nature. The alligators usually keep their distance from the dike that divides the lighthouse freshwater pond from the huge expanse of the Gulf of Mexico. Red cedars and wildflowers line the shores of both these worlds. Saltbush and goldenrod plants on either side of the grass path nourish butterflies that land and sip from flowers. These worlds, the freshwater pond and the saltwater sea are just twenty paces apart. Yet they are as different as Earth and Mars.

The lighthouse at St. Marks National Wildlife Refuge

This place, the St. Marks National Wildlife Refuge, is nature both fine and fierce. There are butterflies and alligators. There are blackberries and black bears. All of this wildlife, from the smallest flower to the largest tree, from a tiny shrimp to a powerful eagle, link together in lifecycles that can repeat for thousands of years.

PROLOGUE

Within all of nature there exists a sense of humor. Of course this comedy is only funny to people because we see in the animals our own human silliness. Penguins walk like Charlie Chaplin. But very few penguins have gone to the movies. So how would they know how to walk in such a peculiar way? Otters slide down slippery rocks for hours on end as if on a playground slide. But otters don't have recess. Are they really having fun? Are monkeys funny or are we laughing at how monkeys and humans are so much alike?

Who is to say what our animal friends truly think and feel? Maybe Nature has a mind of its own. Maybe all the birds and all the bees and butterflies are very aware of what's going on around them, and it is people who simply are not paying attention.

Here are six stories about odd and interesting things that happen throughout the year at the St. Marks Wildlife Refuge. They link together just like the animals and plants at the refuge and in all of nature tend to do. While they may be a stretch of the imagination, it may not be too far a stretch.

ALLIGATORS CAN'T STAND BUTTERFLIES

The alligators living at the St. Marks Wildlife Refuge are not very different from other American alligators in the southeastern United States, who are born and grow to be up to 14 feet long. St. Marks alligators do most of the same things that Louisiana and Georgia alligators do. They snap at anything close by, they snort water out of their nostrils, and roll over in the water as soon as they have something large to eat in their mouths. All alligators spend a great deal of time during the day sleeping. At night they are busy trying to find something to eat. This can be a fish, a duck or even fruit if the tree branches hang low enough. If an alligator snaps at a fish and misses, he ends up with a mouthful of grass and eats it anyway. Alligators are like goats. They will eat just about anything.

Most people think of alligators as being hidden away in the darkest corner of the Okefenokee Swamp, cutting around the canals of the Everglades, or peering out from behind the submerged trunk of a cypress tree deep in a Louisiana bayou. True, there are plenty of alligators in those places. But just as many alligators per acre live at the St. Marks Wildlife Refuge.

As alligator moods and tempers go, perhaps the St. Marks Refuge variety are a bit grumpier than the ones who live in the bayous or the Everglades. This is kind of strange, because the St. Marks Wildlife Refuge would seem a very nice place in which to be an alligator. There's lots of fresh water, there are plenty of fish to eat, and there are warm sandy beaches on the edges of freshwater ponds which are perfect for taking a short six hour nap in the sun.

Alligator napping in the sun

So it is hard to understand why the alligators at the refuge are always so cranky. Still...

It is a little known fact, an arguable truth, but a somewhat accepted idea that St. Marks alligators do not like, will not tolerate, and generally can't stand butterflies. Everyone knows that alligators are, as a rule, quite surly and for the most part disagreeable. They don't get along with the other animals. In fact the preferred way that alligators choose to communicate with their neighbors is simply to sneak up on them and eat them. That is what alligators do best. That, and lounge around in the sun on the sand.

Common moorhen

When an alligator is not sliding quietly through the water trying to sneak up on a white pelican or a common moorhen so as to have it for supper, alligators can usually be seen lying on the sand letting the sun bake heat into their cold blooded and cold hearted bodies.

What is it about butterflies that Alligators particularly despise?

Alligators are always looking for something to swim up behind and eat. They are built for being sneaky. With their dark scaly skin and long round shape, they are easily and often mistaken for just another floating log. In fact that is how alligators catch their dinner. The alligator uses the sharp claws on his webbed feet to scratch at the sand and pull his heavy body into the water. Once launched into the water he moves his long flat tail back and forth, flapping it sideways. The swinging tail propels the alligator ahead rapidly, the legs serving as rudders to steer. Once in position in the water, among the logs and the lily pads, the alligator will then lie very quiet and still in the dark murky water. It will wait for hours or even days if it needs to. Then, when an unfortunate fish under the water or duck paddling on top of the water gets a little too close to that floating log with the two dark glowing ferocious eyes... chomp! The alligator opens his huge mouth, filled with dozens of jagged sharp teeth, and swallows the fish or duck whole.

Alligator fishing

Fortunately most of the ducks and fish are aware that alligators pretend to be logs and they keep a lookout posted all of the time. When one duck sees a suspicious-looking log with yellow-brown eyes and a rounded, bumpy snout, he immediately quacks loudly to warn all of the other ducks. The ducks and other birds nearby lift off from the water and fly away to safety. The alligators simply keep floating around, pretending to be logs, and wait for their next chance to snatch an unsuspecting finned or feathered dinner.

Ducks escaping a hunting alligator

But how does this explain why St. Marks alligators so convincingly and without question hate all the butterflies? Butterflies, especially bright orange Monarch butterflies, make a habit of floating breathlessly on the air. Even a barred owl cannot hear the approach of a floating, slightly fluttering butterfly. An owl can hear a mouse stepping on a twig, but he cannot hear a butterfly floating on the air. So, as sneaky and still as an alligator floating on a pond pretending to be a big brown log might be, he is not nearly as sneaky and quiet as a bright orange Monarch butterfly. And the butterflies seem to know this.

During the middle to end of October each year, there are thousands of Monarch butterflies visiting the St. Marks Wildlife Refuge. At the same time many alligators usually are swimming near the shore of the huge freshwater ponds. The alligators can submerge themselves to the point where they are almost invisible. All you can see of them is a small dark patch of their armored backs and their eyes and snout slightly above

Barred owl

the water's surface. If an alligator is hidden under the water, it is possible to tell its length by guessing the distance from bump on the the tip of his nose to his eyes. Whatever this measures in inches is the length of the alligator in feet.

The Monarch butterflies make a special point of flying over ponds and lagoons looking for big, dumb, unsuspecting alligators. A Monarch will float in low, just above the water, approaching the alligator from behind. The alligator cannot see the orange butterfly because his eyes are facing forward. The butterfly flies along and above the alligator's tail. It skims the air just inches above the alligator's back, and glides along the length of the alligator's long rounded snout. Then, when the gator never suspects it, the butterfly lands directly on the tip of the alligator's nose!

The alligator hates this!

As soon as a butterfly lands on an alligator's nose, the angry gator snaps his huge jaws with a fierce frightening crunch. The ferocious reptile twists in the water, chomping and snapping as fast as he can. The alligator slaps his long powerful tail on the water, lifting himself up so as to try again to eat the butterfly. But the butterfly is too small for an alligator to catch in his fierce jagged teeth.

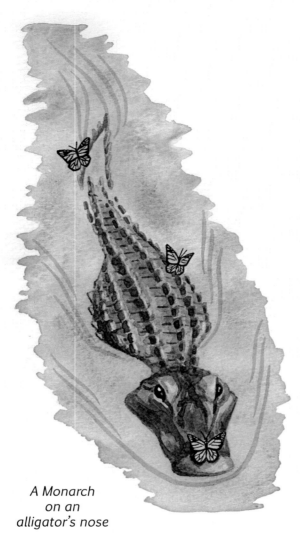

A Monarch on an alligator's nose

Butterflies are surprisingly quick when they want to be… and they always want to be quick when an alligator is angry and trying to eat them. At the moment an alligator uses its tail to push from the water, leap and snap at a butterfly, the butterfly flutters its wings and floats high in the air to safety. An alligator has never once caught a butterfly.

Of course, leaping into the air and snapping their jaws at butterflies draws a great deal of attention. So any ducks or fish that the alligators were trying to sneak up on are instantly alerted. They all fly or swim away to other parts of the pond. And, as if the alligators were not surly and angry enough after waiting for hours trying to catch a fish, having some little orange and black butterflies ruin their chances of eating dinner only makes them madder than ever.

That is why alligators, and in particular the ones at the St. Marks Wildlife Refuge, can't stand butterflies… especially bright orange Monarch butterflies.

Alligators can't stand butterflies!

BUTTERFLIES SOAR AS HIGH AS EAGLES

Eagles are undoubtedly the kings and queens of the skies. They soar to heights above all but the highest clouds. They have eyes with telescopic vision that allow them to spot the smallest of prey from far above. They are so strong that they can dive downward at speeds of over 70 miles per hour to catch a small animal scurrying to shelter or a fish swimming too close to the water's surface. Eagles rule the skies. Their minds are as sharp as their eyes, for an eagle will use the ability of its powerful instinct to find its way to and from faraway places like Maine and Alaska. These powerful aviators, with wings that stretch seven feet across, commute every year to

American Bald Eagle

southern woodlands to escape the cold northern winter snows. American bald eagles have over 7000 blackish-brown and white feathers that are hollow and incredibly light. This lightness and the special curve of their wings allow them to rise high up in the sky on drafts of warm air known as thermals. By tilting themselves downward they move forward, at a flight speed of 30 - 35 miles per hour.

No creature in the sky would dare to threaten an eagle. Their powerful beaks and ripping talons are fiercer than any bird since pterodactyls flew. Eagles are vicious predators that will swiftly swoop down on a flock of migrating ducks or other birds, plucking their dinner from the formation. The huge flocks of ducks moving southward every year to the warm coastal freshwater ponds in Florida all know they must be constantly on the lookout for attack from the single eagles that are also making their way south. Sometimes the ducks fly low with the songbirds to escape the hunger of the eagles. Only the largest geese heading to the sunny states from the upper reaches of Canada are too large for an eagle to pick off one by one, but even the snow geese know better than to fly too near the fearless lone eagle that migrates south at heights of up to 12,000 feet, riding the crest of a tailwind from the fast flowing icy arctic air.

Snow goose

And yet, as the eagle swoops and glides through the air, averaging 30 miles per hour on its trip to meet its mate at their nest in places like the St. Marks Wildlife Refuge along the Florida coastline, it sometimes looks left or right across the sky and sees... a butterfly.

Bald eagle soaring with a Monarch butterfly

The eagle can't believe its telescopic eyes. What on Earth, how could it... what is a butterfly doing up here with me?

The eagle focuses his eyes a little differently. There, flying along with the eagle at an altitude of 11,000 feet above the Earth is not a single butterfly, but thousands of them. The eagle looks farther across the sky, occasionally flapping its powerful wings to keep streaking forward. There, across the sky as far as the superior eyesight of the eagle can see, are hundreds of thousands of bright orange Monarch butterflies.

Monarchs getting ready to liftoff

The Monarchs are on their way south too. At first, there were few of them, as a family of two hundred might lift off from a field filled with milkweed in the Connecticut countryside. Those joined with two hundred more that had been hatched from eggs on milkweed plants in the backyards of homes in northern Ohio. Those four hundred met 2000 Monarch butterflies from Kentucky that had felt the hours of sunlight shorten, telling them to fly away south. Those 2400 joined 10,000 Monarchs from across the American Midwest who took to the air after one late summer night was slightly cooler than the night before.

Monarchs soaring

Those 12,000 plus teamed in the sky with 100,000 Monarchs who left gardens and roadways and meadows from Maine to Minnesota. All of these Monarch butterflies found no new sprouting, growing milkweed to lay their eggs on. So they flew up to the airspace normally reserved only for eagles.

Every year, at summer's end, Monarch butterflies in Canada and the northern United States instinctively leave their gardens filled with marigolds, farms planted with zinnias, and roadside wildflowers, fluttering upward. At first they are simply a few hundred feet in the air, beyond our sight. Then they catch lift from winds busy pushing the clouds across the sky. This carries them up two to three thousand feet, where songbirds such as robins and warblers are flying south for the winter. Finally they reach a level, two miles high in the sky, where powerful

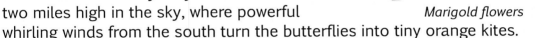

Marigold flowers

whirling winds from the south turn the butterflies into tiny orange kites.

Zinnia

The Monarchs tilt their "sails" slightly downward and surf on the moving air. They needn't flutter their wings. They are constantly diving while the winds, which have gained speed by twisting around the tops of North American mountains constantly keep them aloft. The Monarchs move forward almost as fast as the eagles.

Eagles are as proud as they are fierce. They could never let as insignificant a creature as an insect out-fly them. True, an eagle can fly much faster than a Monarch butterfly, but not any higher. Both the Monarch and the eagle seem unable to fly higher than 12,000 feet. Above that point the air does not have enough oxygen to breathe and is too thin to lift their wings.

So every year, late in summer, a solitary eagle may irritably look over his shoulder at millions of Monarch butterflies that have the nerve to fly as high as an eagle. The eagle catches the wind in the curve of its wings like a sail, and points its beak into a dive, forcing its speed faster and faster.

The butterflies, above the clouds and enjoying the warm sun on their wings and backs, don't know there is a race going on. In fact they can't see more than twenty feet in front of themselves. They find their way south by feeling the angle of the sun's rays on their wings. But the eagle doesn't know that the butterflies aren't racing, and dives deeper into the oncoming wind.

Eventually the sun begins to set and the butterflies notice a chill on their wings. They fly lower to find a cedar or pinewood forest and land for the night. The Monarchs close their wings to gather the warmth in their bodies. Thousands of Monarch butterflies will fall asleep in a single cedar tree. There are hundreds of trees, each filled with the sleeping orange butterflies. The eagle needs to land also. It must find a meal before it can rest and sleep. It cruises low, skimming the landscape, seeking an unsuspecting snack. After its supper the eagle finds a lofty perch to sleep on until morning.

Monarch butterflies resting on a cedar tree branch

The slightest hint of morning light tells the eagle to awaken. It darts upward into the sky as soon as it sees the upper crescent of sun on the eastern horizon. Today the eagle will surely leave those pesky butterflies far behind!

The butterflies yawn and wake slowly, refusing to open their wings until the sun has showered them with warmth. The Monarchs are cold blooded and are not comfortable until the air temperature is at least 60 degrees. The sun must rise and rest its rays on the eastern side of the cedar tree before they will open their wings. Just five more minutes, they tell the cedar tree. Five minutes become an hour. Monarch butterflies are notoriously late sleepers.

The eagle knows that today it will out-fly the butterflies for sure. The huge bird flaps its wings, circling and spiraling upward into the highest reaches of the sky. The morning air is still cool as the eagle loosens up for some high speed wind surfing. After an hour of flying, reaching speeds of almost 60 miles per hour, the sun has risen and the air is warm. The eagle looks ahead to the farthest cloud it can see. How can this be? This can't be. It looks like... this can't be. Somehow, the butterflies are miles ahead of him. How could they possibly have risen and passed him? Yet there they are, each of them alike with their black-bordered bright orange wings, flying south as high as an eagle.

The eagle can't believe his eyes.

BIRDS DON'T LIKE TO BARF

Sure it's easy to believe in the stereotype that birds aren't very smart. Isn't it true that when someone does something a little stupid others may call them a "birdbrain?" Yet birds are much smarter than people realize. There are birds that can talk, birds that can count and even birds that are smart enough not to eat too many fried foods. Those are birds that live in homes as pets or in the city as well... pigeons, actually. But out in the woods and the wild of the St. Marks Refuge, the birds are smart in other ways. When a storm is coming the birds know to find shelter in their nest or the hollow of a tree. Should a bird be too big to fit in one of those places, as in the case of wading birds

Anhinga

such as great blue herons and great egrets, these birds know just where to hide to stay comfortable. Birds of this type sometimes take shelter under palm fronds and other large leaves but herons, egrets and most of the other birds that live in the salt and freshwater marshes along the shore usually don't mind the rain at all. Their feathers produce natural oils and when their wings are closed this makes them mostly waterproof. The smartest of these wading birds make the best of a wet opportunity by doing a little fishing or crabbing during the rain. Birds such as anhingas and herons are the greatest fishermen in the world. Although most of their fishing is done during daylight hours, great blue herons may sometimes stand in a pond on a moonlit night, watching for the shining of a fish's back as it swims near the surface of the water. On sunny days these smart birds catch dozens of tiny shrimp and crabs among the marsh reeds. And when it rains, herons don't go fishing at all. Instead they feast on an endless supply of toads hopping out of the woods and into the rain to escape the heat of summer.

Heron chasing a hopping toad

The wading birds of St. Marks not only know what to eat, they know what not to eat as well. The first thing birds learn after they hatch in their nests at St. Marks is not to eat the butterflies. At least not the orange ones with the black markings. They can eat all the yellow Cloudless Sulphur butterflies, blue Spring Azure butterflies and brown Carolina Satyr butterflies they want. In fact, to a bird these are as tasty as potato chips. But whatever a bird does, it must never eat the bright orange and black Monarch butterflies.

Cloudless Sulphur butterfly

Spring Azure butterfly

Monarch butterflies begin their life as Monarch caterpillars. These yellow and black tiger-striped fellows are born from eggs right onto their favorite food, milkweed plants. The very second they hatch, these tiny Monarch caterpillars begin chomping away at the soft green milkweed leaves. In just three weeks, the Monarch caterpillars have grown to be big, plump bugs, seemingly a tasty treat for a bird. We say seemingly because these little fellows have been eating, and building strong little bug bodies with milkweed. And milkweed is, for most creatures, poisonous. Monarch caterpillars have developed immunity to the poison, and store the poison in their bodies.

Monarch caterpillar

When the caterpillar is five weeks old, he or she knows it is time to become a butterfly. First, it must seal itself away inside a green chrysalis. A chrysalis is a shell-like covering that the caterpillar builds and will live in while quietly turning into a butterfly. When the transformation is complete, the new butterfly will split open the now transparent chrysalis shell.

When it emerges from its chrysalis, it is a full-fledged Monarch butterfly with all of the special black markings and white spots on its bright orange wings. And all of that poison from the milkweed that the caterpillar ate is now built into its wings and the shell of its body.

The poison content built up in one little Monarch butterfly from all of those milkweed leaves it ate as a caterpillar is strong enough to give a heart attack to a bird or any other animal that eats it. Fortunately when birds do eat the Monarchs, they are able to get the poison out of their bellies in a hurry before it makes them very ill.

Not all of the birds that are born at the wildlife refuge are aware that they should positively never eat Monarch butterflies. Remember, some birds are smarter than others. And other birds just won't listen to reason when they think they are going to eat hundreds of tasty butterfly chip treats. Those birds, who probably started the habit of people calling birds "birdbrains" refuse to pay attention during the orientation and training sessions held every year. No doubt they were staring out at the blue gulf waters when the older wiser birds explained that they should never eat the orange Monarch butterflies.

Adult Pelican teaching the younger birds

As is always the case, many young teenage birds only pretend to be listening to their parents when they explain about the poisoned insects.

Young ibis eating a Monarch butterfly

Birds, like people, must sometimes learn their lessons the hard way. At the St. Marks Wildlife Refuge this happens at the end of every summer and the beginning of every fall. There are thousands of coastal birds living at the refuge. Almost all of them know better than to eat the poisonous Monarch butterflies. But every year when the butterflies start arriving from northern climates, quite a few young great blue herons, brown pelicans, white ibis and great egrets think they are smarter than all the other birds and feast on the Monarch butterflies. No, these birds won't get sick and die from eating the Monarch butterflies. But they do pay dearly for not paying attention.

About an hour after an egret, pelican or other St. Marks wading bird has stuffed himself with Monarch butterflies, that bird starts to notice that its stomach feels very funny. It feels more than funny, it feels really sick. Oh, they try to pretend they are fine by sipping water and strolling around in the ponds, but anyone who takes a look at them can tell they are not feeling well. You wouldn't think that a great blue heron could turn green or that a white ibis could look yellow, but a few hours after eating the Monarch butterflies, these birds are ill to the gills.

Birds, people, fish and just about every animal in the world share one trait and behavior. When something lands in their stomach that their body doesn't like, their stomach tries to get rid of it.

There are two ways that chewed poisonous Monarch butterflies can leave a pelican or other bird's body. They can go up or they can go down. They usually go up.

Young pelicans tossing their Monarch butterfly cookies

Those foolish pelicans that ate the Monarch butterflies all hang their heads off the end of the remains of the St. Marks pier, tossing their Monarch butterfly cookies. The herons, with their long necks, try to hide in the tall reeds, pretending they are hunting for fish, but everyone can hear them coughing up chunks of bright orange wings. Don't think the egrets fare any better. They hack and hurl so violently that the mallards and wood ducks in the middle of the ponds have to... well, duck! It is an ugly mess with all those young stupid birds barfing up butterflies all across the freshwater ponds.

Eventually all the bird-brained birds have expelled the poisonous butterflies from their stomachs. Those same birds will sit real still during the month that the Monarch butterflies visit the St. Marks Wildlife Refuge. Very often, if a bird who got sick eating butterflies even sees another Monarch, it starts to throw up all over again! Most of them never eat another butterfly for the rest of their lives.

The next year, once again new young birds are hatched at the refuge, who don't know the dangers of eating the Monarch butterflies. The egrets, pelicans and herons who got sick to their stomachs the year before try to warn them. But once again, some of the young birds refuse to listen. And all the animals living near the ponds get ready to "duck" and take cover.

Duck and take cover!

ARE DRAGONFLIES TINY DRAGONS?

It's hard to say whether dragons are as fierce as people claim them to be. The general belief and rumor is that dragons are extremely large, have huge bat-like wings, breathe fire and will eat anything or anyone they don't especially like. Furthermore, the history of dragons seems to point out that no dragon ever liked anyone. That is, with the exception of that rascal Puff.* Of course we can't say for sure whether dragons were nice or not because there don't seem to be any flying around. In fairness to the dragons, we should not assume they were horrible frightening creatures. Perhaps, for the most part, they were quite polite.

Blue dasher dragonfly

Now dragonflies are another matter. There are plenty of these fellows around and they make no effort to hide their disposition. They show their general unfriendliness by biting just about any other insect they can sink their tiny sharp teeth into. Fortunately they don't bite people, for dragonflies have teeth like dinosaurs, only smaller of course. Dragonflies prefer to bite into flying ants, honeybees, and Monarch butterflies. But they will eat mosquitoes if they have to, when nothing better to eat is flying in the air.

Flying ant

Flying ant

Just as with butterflies, there are hundreds of different kinds of dragonflies. And the St. Marks Wildlife Refuge is home for many of them. Many people collect pictures of dragonflies, and think that dragonflies are just as beautiful as butterflies. Butterflies laugh at this notion, for they believe nothing is as beautiful as they are. At the St. Marks Wildlife Refuge there are four main types of dragonflies in residence. They have names like four-spotted pennants, roseate skimmers, blue dashers, and pond hawks. These flying insects zip through the air so quickly that our eyes can scarcely follow them, and they are almost always named for their actions. Skimmers skim the water, dashers are super fast and pond hawks... both the bright green female pondhawks and the deep blue males, are the most dangerous type of dragonfly, if you happen to be a delicious honeybee.

"Puff the magic dragon lived by the sea...

Little Jackie Paper loved that rascal Puff..."

Honeybee

Honeybees tend to stay safe in their hives and flying ants live deep inside their nests, so most of the year the dragonflies living in the reeds along the watery marshes have to eat mosquitoes. This is a great help for the rangers who work in the refuge and the people who visit. In fact, if the dragonflies would simply acquire a taste for and learn to like to eat mosquitoes, everyone would be better off... especially the butterflies. There are always way too many mosquitoes everywhere and dragonflies could be heroes if they simply chose to eat them. But they won't, unless they are too hungry and none of the things they like to eat better are flying around. And they seldom are. Except... once a year, beginning in October, when tens of thousands of Monarch butterflies decide to fly south for the winter.

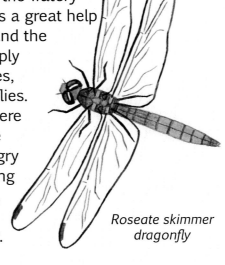

Roseate skimmer dragonfly

From spring through summer, female Monarch butterflies lay eggs on milkweed plants all across America. From those eggs hatch tiny Monarch caterpillars who gobble up milkweed leaves as fast as they can for three to four weeks. At the end of that time, the caterpillar hides itself away inside a special wrapping called a chrysalis. After two more weeks a beautiful Monarch butterfly emerges from the chrysalis shell. That butterfly soon lays its own eggs on a milkweed plant and the cycle of life for Monarch caterpillars and butterflies begins once again. This cycle repeats itself many times from May until September.

Monarch caterpillar eating a milkweed leaf

Monarch chrysalis and butterfly

Asters

At summer's end, the last generation of Monarch butterflies for that year stops laying eggs. The Monarchs notice the days of summer growing shorter in length. They feel the chill of night air that comes as fall approaches. Also the flowers they prefer to sip nectar from such as goldenrods, dandelions, asters and marigolds, all tend to wither and die in early autumn. The Monarchs read the signs of the season's change. Those signs can be as subtle as a wilted flower or harsh as an early frost.

Every year, as summer dwindles down to the days when children, who had spent the summer blowing the seeds from dandelions, dread the coming return of school, the Monarch butterflies from all of the northern United States, and Canada feel the chill of the morning air and without any notice to their friends and favorite flowers, fly away toward warmer places. The Monarchs, with their bright orange wings with black veins and white spots, who had been perfectly content floating about northern summer gardens and meadows, leave the total comfort of their summer homes in Connecticut, Maine or Minnesota, beginning a journey of over one thousand miles.

Dandelions

Unlike most butterflies that only flap their wings and flutter about, Monarchs have the ability to soar. They glide as high up in the sky as can the geese and mallard ducks. They fly south on jet winds high above the robins, warblers and other songbirds. The Monarchs fly with the eagles from faraway places like Bangor, Maine. And just like the much bigger migrating birds, the Monarchs stop to rest. Geese, ducks and eagles breathe a sigh of relief when they finally reach their winter home at the St. Marks Wildlife Refuge. The eagles, who return every year, have nests from the year before that welcome them. They settle in for a warm Florida winter where they can catch plenty of food and raise their

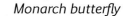

Monarch butterfly

young. The Monarch butterflies only stay for a few days to rest. For the Monarchs, this stop is just a Florida motel where they will soak in the poolside sun. When the Monarchs leave St. Marks, most will travel to the place that almost all of the North American Monarch butterflies call their ancestral home. This is in the mountain valleys in central Mexico. The late summer last generation of Monarch butterflies can somehow find this spot without ever having been there before. The yearly butterfly journey doesn't end until the Monarchs from all across North America reach the town of Angangueo and the forest valleys of the Sierra Madre Mountains deep in central Mexico. Until then, all of their days are filled with danger.

Monarch butterfly

One of those dangers is the dragonflies. Monarch butterfly bodies are filled with poison from the diet of milkweed leaves they ate as caterpillars. Unfortunately for the butterflies, dragonflies are immune to the poison. After a summer of eating mosquito after mosquito, the dragonflies hungrily await the October arrival of the Monarch butterflies at St. Marks. They swarm around the tall white St. Marks lighthouse, waiting for the butterflies to warm themselves in the sun. Most of the Monarchs manage to spend their time at St. Marks safely resting in the branches of cedar trees and sipping nectar from the saltbush flowers before following the shore along the Gulf of Mexico and reaching their genetic home.

Four-spotted pennant dragonfly

Goldenrod

But a few of the Monarchs are taken by the dragonflies. Some fly too slowly, weary from the long trip south. Others are simply in the air at the wrong time, while attempting to move from the cover of the cedar trees to the safety of a soft bunch of blossoms. Dragonflies attack from the air and in the air. If a butterfly or a honeybee can successfully land on a bush or a flower, it will usually be safe. But butterflies are not too quick as they flutter from the trees where they sleep, to breakfast on the goldenrod blossoms. And a dragonfly is much faster and can turn in the air more quickly than any Monarch butterfly.

There are many people in the world who truly believe that dragons still exist and are merely living in hiding. If the dragons are laying low, then perhaps all that has been written about them is false. Perhaps, for the most part, dragons were simply misunderstood. Until one decides to show itself, people will never be sure. What we do know is that for the Monarch butterflies resting at the St. Marks Wildlife Refuge, some tiny dragons are very, very real.

Pond hawk dragonfly

Are dragonflies tiny dragons?

DO BEARS SNEEZE IN THE WOODS?

A Florida black bear needs around 20,000 acres of woods to wander in order to feel at home. Like all bears, the Florida kind like to roam around looking for food and doing a little exploring. As recently as 100 years ago when most of Florida was a wilderness, there was plenty of room for black bears to roam large territories. Today the land available for bear habitat is just enough to support 3000 round-eared Florida bears. The stomping ground of a black bear community can overlap with other bears but the average black bear population still needs around 1000 acres per member to survive. This means that the entire St. Marks Wildlife Refuge with 68,000 acres is probably home to no more than 70 Florida black bears.

Florida black bear

Much is known about Florida black bears including the ones that live at St. Marks. Unlike their fierce grizzly bear cousins, Florida bears are actually very shy, so seeing one while walking in the woods is unlikely. They are exceptionally cute with very round fuzzy ears. They are all black except for their brown snouts that are a bit longer than snouts belonging to most other types of bears. There is an expression among bears that has been true for hundreds of years, "The longer the snout, the better the sniff."

Tupelo berries

This is apparently so, for Florida black bears rely upon their noses to guide them in many ways. Florida bears spend most of their time hunting for honey and berries and other good things to eat. They use their powerful sense of smell to find saw palmetto berries, acorns and occasionally tupelo berries. If something is good to eat, a bear's nose can find it.

Most people are completely unaware that when these bears are not busy foraging for food, their favorite pastime just happens to be... sniffing flowers. Unlike people, who never seem to have time to smell the flowers along the way, Florida black bears make a particular point of doing so. A typical bear might be walking in the woods, pushing and shoving his way through the heavy palmetto scrub, when the scent of wild honeysuckle blossoms comes drifting right into his snout. Unless the bear is already engaged in a more important pursuit, such as scratching his back on the bark of a tree or that other thing bears are noted for doing in the woods, he will immediately hurry off in the direction of the fragrance.

Florida black bear sniffing flowers

The olfactory sense, or smelling ability of an American black bear, of which the Florida species are a part, is about 50 times that of a person. So a bear might take particular pleasure in smelling the pine lilies, pickerel weed, or sweet bay flowers growing at the St. Marks Refuge.

Pine lily

Female Florida black bears have even longer, more slender snouts than the males. These are perfect for flower sniffing, but not all of a bear's sniffing is strictly recreational. Most of the time they are using that powerful ability to locate food. They sniff along the ground and high into the air trying to catch a whiff of food on the wind. Black bears can, if they have a reason and are of a mind to, climb trees. If a bear smells a clump of berries or a hive full of honey bees high on a branch of a tree, the bear will shinny up the trunk to reach them. The bears like to eat the bees almost as much as they like the honey.

Honeycomb

For their hobby of flower sniffing, the bears of St. Marks are limited mostly to sniffing the flowers growing along the ground. Besides the few flowers mentioned that are favorite bear nosegays, the bears of St. Marks especially enjoy sniffing the flowers of frost asters, pickerel weed, and cardinal flowers. It is these wild flowers that sometimes get the bears into trouble.

Near the shoreline of the Gulf of Mexico, along the area known as "The Forgotten Coast," grow an abundant assortment of native wild flowers. They bloom in dozens of magnificent colors such as day flower blue, cardinal flower red, drum-heads pink, and horse nettle lavender. Unlike most animals in the forest, black bears are not color blind. Deer and raccoons and possums cannot tell red from green and purple from maroon, but bears are able to see all the colors of the rainbow.

Pickerel weed

Bumble bee

The bears appreciate all the different wildflower fragrances and all of the beautiful colors nature wraps them in, but the very favorite of Florida black bears seems to be ...goldenrod. In Florida, during the early fall, these wildflowers that many people consider to be a weed, bloom in abundance. Goldenrod plants at the St. Marks Refuge routinely grow to be 3 feet tall or taller. Each plant has hundreds of tiny bright yellow flowers, each brimming with nectar. Honey bees and bumble bees love the nectar from goldenrod as do all types of butterflies.

Starting in October, hundreds of goldenrod bushes at the St. Marks Refuge begin to bloom. Around that same time, thousands of Monarch butterflies arrive in Florida from long journeys that began hundreds of miles away. The butterflies are on their way to Mexico to hibernate through the winter. But first they must rest up and gather their strength by drinking plenty of nectar from the yellow goldenrod and greenish-gray saltbush flowers. Monarch butterflies drink and enjoy all types of flower nectar. One of their favorites just happens to be nectar from the bright yellow goldenrod flowers.

Monarch butterfly drinking saltbush flower nectar

Humans, for the most part, consider goldenrod to be a horrible annoyance. For some, it makes their eyes water and their noses sneeze constantly. It makes the bears sneeze also, but bears don't mind sneezing. It seems a good sneeze can do wonders to clear up a clogged snout. In fact, for Florida black bears, that is the main enticement of the goldenrod flowers. It's amazing how much stuff bears can suck up into their noses while sniffing along the ground. Flower seeds, pieces of pine needles, tiny chips of bark and dozens of other forest floor ingredients somehow get stuck in bears' snouts. The chance to clear out any bits of berries or fur that happen to get lodged in their noses is completely irresistible. A single clump of goldenrod can hold a thousand tiny flowers and because bears just love sniffing flowers and getting a chance to blow their noses... goldenrod can be very useful.

*Monarch butterflies
sipping goldenrod nectar*

The bears at St. Marks rarely leave the cover and safety of their wooded areas. And goldenrod generally doesn't grow deep in the woods. But every so often a heavy stormy wind picks up a clump of dried goldenrod flowers with the seeds attached, carries them through the air and drops them into a clear spot in the middle of the woods. Light filters down to earth through openings in the branches of the trees. The seeds start to grow and the roots dig into the ground quite comfortably. By the time spring and summer have passed, a full grown three-foot-tall goldenrod bush is situated in the middle of the woods, with sunlight gleaming off its bright yellow flowers.

When something is most unlikely to happen, that's when it usually does. So from time to time in late October, a Florida black bear will walk into a tiny clearing in the forest and come upon a goldenrod bush, just bursting with fragrant beautiful bright yellow flowers. Not wanting to let such a wonderful opportunity pass, the bear will plunge her snout into the flowers to take a long deep sniff of their fragrance. The bear is always so happy to have stumbled upon her favorite flower that she never takes notice of the three or four Monarch butterflies silently sipping nectar from those same yellow flowers. What happens next happens so fast that no one is to blame. Paying no attention to anything but the flowers, the bear takes a huge breath and sniffs way too much pollen into her nose. The butterflies are so busy drinking nectar they don't notice the nose of the bear. The pollen itches and twitches inside the snout of the bear. Her eyes start to water. The bear's nose explodes in a fur-ious sneeze. Flowers, fur, berry bits and Monarch butterflies are blown everywhere. Fortunately no one is hurt. The blast, though powerful, lasts only an instant. The bear's nose is cleaned out and as good as new. And the butterflies... are well on their way to Mexico.

The bear's nose explodes in a fur-ious sneeze.

BUTTERFLIES FLY AWAY

Every night for over 150 years, the beacon of the St. Marks lighthouse has been shining its light outward into the Gulf of Mexico, defeating the curve of the earth from its high perch above the land. The lofty placement of the lamp allows ships' captains at sea to spot the light from as far away as 50 miles and steer safely along the Florida coast. During daylight hours the lamp is turned off and visitors can tour the grounds surrounding the ancient and famous St. Marks lighthouse. Not all of the visitors are people.

St. Marks lighthouse shining at night

Red cedar tree branch with berries

In early October, thousands of Monarch butterflies begin to arrive at the St. Marks Wildlife Refuge. For the most part, they rest and sleep in the branches of the soft red cedar trees that line the shore near the lighthouse. Some of the Monarchs have traveled just a few days journey from places like the Blue Ridge Mountains. Others have soared for almost a month, beginning their trip from as far away as Ontario, Canada. They are almost to their winter home in warm sunny central Mexico, or perhaps in south Florida or the Bahamas. Somehow they found their way here to the St. Marks Wildlife Refuge where last year the great-great-grand parents of these Monarch butterflies also stopped to rest.

How did they find their way? And how do they know where they are going? The butterflies carry within their being a secret map, passed on to them from all the generations of Monarchs who lived before them. That map and the rays of the sun guide them down all of North America. It reminds them where the best forests are to stop and rest. It warns them to land and drink and sleep before crossing large lakes and seas. The map in their genetic history tells them how to find the St. Marks Wildlife Refuge.

It almost seems as if the Monarchs can see the bright white-painted St. Marks lighthouse from the bright blue skies above. They really cannot see that far away, but with a stored genetic instinct map inside of them they don't need to see the lighthouse. They already know it is there.

Generally by the fourth Saturday in October, most of the Monarch butterflies resting on layover at St. Marks have arrived. They have spent days lounging about in the Florida sun, soaking up warmth while sipping nectar from the brilliant yellow goldenrod and light greenish-gray saltbush flowers that line the paths along the shore. For exercise and to stay loose until the last leg of their trip to Mexico, the Monarchs at the St. Marks Refuge will flitter from one bunch of flowers to the next, sipping nectar here and there as if one flower's beverage might be sweeter than the other.

Monarch butterflies finding their way to St. Marks lighthouse

Many people believe the Monarch butterflies are simply following their instinct by stopping to rest at St. Marks, but there are just as many and maybe secretly more who know in their hearts that the butterflies are completely aware of everything they do.

Monarch butterflies are extremely odd insects. As you know, they like to tease alligators, race eagles and hate alarm clocks. They don't like to be sneezed on by bears and they are rightfully terrified of tiny flying dragons. And when swallowed by foolish birds, Monarch butterflies have been known to exact a very special kind of revenge. Still, one would say that butterflies in general and Monarchs in particular are friendly to everyone they meet. Butterflies never bite. And they love to entertain.

The rangers who run the St. Marks Wildlife Refuge and all of the animals who live there (with the exception of the alligators) all make a special welcome for the visiting Monarch butterflies. Gardeners plant and transplant the butterflies' favorite flowers all year round. The Florida black bears make a special effort not to blow away too many blossoms while sniffing flowers. The great blue herons tell the brown pelicans who remind the snowy egrets who warn the wood ducks and snow geese not to eat the Monarchs, lest everyone suffer. The dragonflies... well, no, they are still just plain mean. But everyone else involved readies the wildlife refuge for these once-a-year special visitors.

It seems only fair then, that during the month of October, and especially on Saturdays, that the Monarchs of St. Marks should be a little more sociable and in some instances even friendly. On Saturday mornings when most Monarch butterflies prefer to "sleep in," the St. Marks visitors all wake up and stretch their wings as soon as the first glance of sunlight has risen above the trees to the east. This first bit of dawn light sends patches of warmth onto the blossoming goldenrod and saltbush plants, as well as all of the other flowers in full autumn bloom on the refuge.

As the sun rises higher and the air becomes warmer, the Monarchs all leave the shelter of the warm red cedars. By 10 a.m., all of the bushes and trees that bear autumn flowers are covered in light and all of the flowers on them are covered in Monarch butterflies. There are thousands of the orange, black and white Monarchs. Most are sipping nectar so as to build strength to fly around the Gulf of Mexico to... Mexico. The rest, as part of an overall attitude of friendliness, are flying around the St. Marks lighthouse for the amusement and entertainment of the hundreds of people who also decided not to sleep in, woke extra early, and drove to the wildlife refuge specifically to see the butterflies. Monarchs are everywhere. They hover next to the white painted bricks of the lighthouse just so that people can take photographs of them with a background that shows off their colors. They cluster on bunches of flowers in groups of fifteen and twenty. When a person quietly slips up on them with camera in hand to take a photograph, the Monarchs all open their wings and sit quietly as they sip flower nectar, so that the pictures never turn out blurry...well, almost never. By just after lunchtime, there are almost as many people circling the lighthouse as there are Monarch butterflies. This makes for a close but friendly environment. Usually there aren't enough places for people or butterflies to rest upon, so some of the Monarchs save space by landing on the arms, shoulders and heads of children. Fortunately butterflies never bite, though they have been known to tickle.

In the same way that the late summer chill caused the butterflies to shiver and scrunch their wings while they were up north, the onset of autumn in the Florida panhandle reminds the Monarch butterflies that they now must finish their journey. They wake with the sun, warm their wings and simply flit to the sky from their cedar tree branches. In clusters of fourteen to twenty or groups of two or four, the Monarchs allow the breeze wafting across the warm gulf waters to lift them. Sometimes the entire population of a tree will leave at once, all together. The balmy moving air swirls and twirls the feather-light Monarchs upward with little direction. But they quickly feel the rays of the sun and all turn towards the sea. Any people visiting the lighthouse on those days squint their eyes or use binoculars to see the butterflies for every second that they can. Soon they cannot, as the butterflies flutter and soar higher. The Monarchs climb on the air to five, ten, and eleven thousand feet of altitude where winds coming from the direction they are heading to, turn them into little boats, bright boats with glimmering orange and black sails, gliding across the sky, high above the Gulf of Mexico.

In seven days the Monarchs will be safe in their winter home. The Monarchs from St. Marks will join two million other Monarchs who have come from all across North America to sleep and rest in the Oyamel fir trees of Mexico. There they will half-hibernate, like Florida bears, until spring.

The Monarchs all turn toward the sea.